TAKE
CONTROL
of the
NOISY
CLASS
Workbook

ROB PLEVIN

LIFERAFTMEDIA Ltd

Published by
Life Raft Media Ltd www.liferaftmedia.com
Copyright Rob Plevin 2020

Print ISBN: 978-1-913514-09-9
Kindle ISBN: 978-1-913514-10-5
eBook/Other: 978-1-913514-11-2

CONTENTS

ABOUT THIS WORKBOOK

This workbook will help you bring to life in your classrooms the ideas and techniques laid out in *Take Control of the Noisy Class.*

Its aim is to help teachers and support staff to improve their effectiveness in the classroom using the Needs Focused Teaching philosophy.

Each of the 13 chapters in the book is structured into 5 main sections:

1. **Resources**. This section provides page references for relevant material in *Take Control of the Noisy Class.* Where applicable, additional Needs Focused resources, such as videos and books, will also be listed.

2. **Key concepts**. These are the main ideas and critical understandings in each phase of the Needs Focused Classroom Management process.

3. **Focus questions**. These questions guide your reading of *Take Control of the Noisy Class* as a basis for personal reflection, or for discussion during weekly Study Group meetings (see below).

4. **Activities**. The activities provide opportunity to delve deeper into, and practise, implementing the skills, techniques and ideas outlined in *Take Control of the Noisy Class* and associated resources, through a variety of tasks and scenarios.

5. **Share your ideas**. Here you have the opportunity to contribute (and receive feedback on) your suggestions and answers in a private forum, along with other readers of the workbook.

In some chapters an additional section is provided: **Additional Reading**. This section, where relevant, provides extra background information on the techniques being taught.

There is an optional **Initial Assessment** at the start of the book and a final **Review Assessment** at the end, to gauge progress made using the materials.

Why not study with friends & colleagues?

Getting familiar with, and practising, the various Needs Focused strategies contained in *Take Control of the Noisy Class* is a lot easier with a little help from your friends and colleagues. A study group can provide the perfect environment in which to rehearse and perfect your classroom management skills.

A brief after-school or pre-school meeting can become a great source of new skills and affordable staff development—with feedback and input from fellow professionals helping all attendees find solutions to difficult problems and situations.

How to run a Study Group

The activities and questions in this workbook can be adapted to provide structure for 13 main study group meetings (of roughly 45 minutes duration) followed by an optional, ongoing weekly session. This weekly session can either be a refresher meeting to recap previous sessions or a 'Behaviour Surgery' to focus on classroom behaviour problems, such as those highlighted in Chapter 13 of *Take Control of the Noisy Class* or site-specific issues.

The 13 study group meetings will focus on the following key Needs Focused Teaching areas:

1. Classroom management essentials

2. Establishing routines

3. Giving clear instructions

4. Consequences

5. Positive teacher-student relationships

6. Positive reinforcement

7. Taking control at the door

8. Seating plans

9. Getting them into the room—the filter method

10. Getting the lesson started

11. Maintaining a positive learning environment

12. Maintaining lesson flow

13. Dealing with problems

Behaviour Surgery (Meetings 14+):

Dealing with common problems

Dealing with site-specific issues

Meeting Structure

As well as discussing the key concepts, answering the focus questions and completing the activities for each chapter, some additional activities for study group meetings are provided in the appendix. These can help turn a short after-school or pre-school meeting into a practical, hands-on workshop.

INITIAL ASSESSMENT:

My progress as a Needs Focused teacher

Rank each statement by circling a number between 1 (low) and 10 (high).

I have a positive attitude towards my students and my teaching	1 2 3 4 5 6 7 8 9 10
I have routines in place to automate my classroom and make transitions run smoothly	1 2 3 4 5 6 7 8 9 10
I make a priority of building positive relationships with my students and making each of them feel valued	1 2 3 4 5 6 7 8 9 10
I focus on positive classroom management by acknowledging a praising appropriate behaviour	1 2 3 4 5 6 7 8 9 10
I have high expectations for all my students	1 2 3 4 5 6 7 8 9 10
My students are calm and settled at the start of my lessons	1 2 3 4 5 6 7 8 9 10
I make sure to give clear instructions in a calm manner, phrased so that my students will understand them	1 2 3 4 5 6 7 8 9 10
I know how to establish and maintain a positive learning environment	1 2 3 4 5 6 7 8 9 10
I know how to maintain lesson flow in order to minimise disruption and misbehaviour	1 2 3 4 5 6 7 8 9 10
I know how to deliver consequences without causing animosity	1 2 3 4 5 6 7 8 9 10
I have a range of specific responses for the most common classroom behaviour problems	1 2 3 4 5 6 7 8 9 10
I know how to start over with a very difficult class	1 2 3 4 5 6 7 8 9 10

Use this table to compare your starting point with your progress at the end of the book in your journey to making an impact on your students. At the end of this workbook you will be asked to reflect on your journey and compare the results with the table you complete today.

1. CLASSROOM MANAGEMENT ESSENTIALS

Resources

Take Control of the Noisy Class   Pages: 1–31

Additional Resources

Needs Focused Classroom Management Video pack.   Videos 1–4: Attitude
SAVE £150–Discounted access for workbook buyers.
Get the videos in digital form here for just £47 (normally £197):
https://needsfocusedteaching.com/video-packwbd

Key concepts

- Effective teaching starts with the attitude of the teacher.

- Preventing problems is easier than having to deal with them.

- The way we respond to students will determine how they react.

- Young people need teachers to be consistent–it's not what teachers do to deal with mis-behaviour that characterises effective classroom management, but how they prevent problems in the first place.

Focus Questions

1. What sort of issues might lead to problem behaviour in a classroom? (p 14)

2. What are some of the characteristics of a vigilant teacher? (pp 16-19)

3. What would consistency look like when it is being applied on a daily basis? (pp 19-22)

4. How can keeping detailed records help you when dealing with a parent/guardian or another member of staff? (p 23)

5. Describe a time when you were in a business/work environment that was not well-managed or in which people had a negative attitude. How did it make you feel? Did the experience influence the rest of your day? How might you apply your answers to your teaching?

Activities

ACTIVITY 1 – Preventive classroom management

Preventative strategies are the foundation of Needs Focused Classroom Management. By eliminating (or at least minimising) the likely underlying causes of student behaviour problems, life in the classroom can be made calmer and more enjoyable while teaching and learning can be improved.

Step #1 – Identify possible reasons for inappropriate behaviour

Choose one class or group of students you teach regularly for this exercise. Your task is to write down TWO behaviour challenges you most frequently experience with this group and then consider what might be causing these to occur. Use the table below or similar to record your answers.

NB We can't always be 100% sure what is driving observed behaviours – sometimes the best we can do is take a good guess. But the idea of this exercise is simply to look at situations from your students' point of view. Once you start making a habit of this, you'll be surprised how reliable your best guesses can be. If you're unsure or have no idea at all at this stage as to what may be the cause of the behaviour you're witnessing, don't worry; it may well become more apparent in due course. And while it certainly helps to know specifically what is behind the various behaviour problems we encounter in the classroom, it's not essential in terms of general strategies for preventing them, nor for addressing them in a non-confrontational manner.

Asking your students directly what *they* feel is the cause of inappropriate behaviour is often a good way to get the answers you need, and in a later exercise we will examine how to conduct a student meeting to facilitate this as part of a Fresh Start initiative. For now though, just have a rough guess as to what you feel may be the possible reasons behind their actions. You may be surprised how obvious it is to *uncover* likely causes once you take a step back and start thinking about the various problems when you're not engrossed in actually dealing with them.

Problem	Possible causes	Preventive Solutions
Constant chatter	1. Too much emphasis on 'teacher talk' during lessons. 2. Slow pace of activities. 3. Not enough variety or challenge in activities. 4. Not dealing with perpetrators quickly enough and allowing minor disruptions to go unchallenged. 5. Consequences not clearly defined or consistently applied.	

Step #2 – Identify preventive solutions

If some of the underlying reasons for the behaviours you're encountering are obvious to you now, you can make plans to prevent them happening. Fill in your answers in the 'Preventive Solutions' column.

For example, in terms of addressing the causes of constant chatter (my example in the table above, I might add the following Preventive Solutions:

1. *Keep my explanations and introductions to a minimum, perhaps providing written/pictorial instructions where appropriate.*

2. *Get students straight into some hands-on activity and perhaps include discussion activities of some kind (these students like to talk, right?).*

3. *Have a selection of alternative activities on stand-by as well as extension work. Maintain a brisk pace throughout each stage of the lesson as well as through transitions.*

4. *Be more vigilant and address minor infractions as soon as possible to avoid noise levels escalating. Remind students of the classroom rules and consequences. I would NOT do this at the start of a lesson when it may set a negative tone for the rest of our time together; it is better to wait until students are in a positive frame of mind. Establish routines for maintaining appropriate noise levels and smooth transitions.*

5. *Consistency in upholding rules and delivery of consequences.*

Share your ideas

Share your answers in the **Classroom Management Success FB group** with a heading: **'Preventing Problems'**.

You can join the group here:
https://www.facebook.com/groups/Classroommanagementsuccess

ACTIVITY 2 – Classroom Management Essentials

Step #1. Cast your mind back to one or two recent classroom behaviour problems you've encountered with a group of students or a particularly challenging individual. In the table below write these in the 'Incident' column.

Step #2. Write down how you might have used any or all of the methods from pages 13-25 (listed below) to help avoid or improve the situation. If you're brand new to teaching you can do this exercise by thinking how these same methods will help you with your classes in future.

- Have the right attitude

- Be vigilant

- Remain calm

- Start with the least disruptive intervention

- Be consistent

- Show respect

- Divide and conquer

- Keep a detailed record of the event

- Project control

- Avoid nagging or lecturing

- Utilise your support network

Incident	How might the situation have been improved?

ACTIVITY 3 – The Needs Focused Teacher

Use the information found on pages 1-10 (Introduction) as well as the key Classroom Management Essentials mentioned on pages 13-25 to annotate the diagram below with the features and characteristics you feel to be most indicative of a Needs Focused Teacher. How would a Needs Focused Teacher communicate with her students? What sort of teaching skills would she employ? What activities might she present to her students? What sort of responses might she use when confronted with behaviour problems in her classroom? How does she facilitate excellence in teaching and learning?

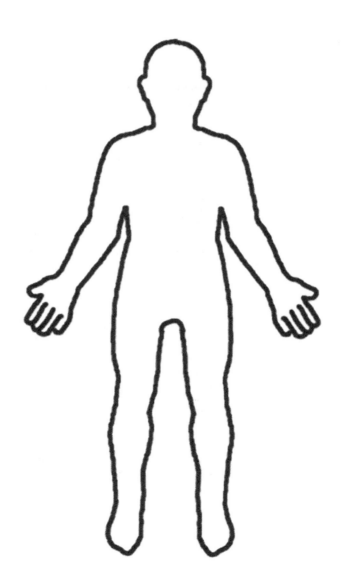

Share your ideas

Share your features and ideas in the **Classroom Management Success FB group** with a heading: **'The Needs Focused Teacher'**.

You can join the group here:
https://www.facebook.com/groups/Classroommanagementsuccess

ACTIVITY 4 – Your Support System

Support systems are critical to creating a sense of confidence for teachers. It can feel tremendously reassuring to know that you have people, plans and resources in place to assist you in meeting your classroom management goals and in handling particularly challenging situations. But where do you begin? In this activity, you will 'mind-map' how to create a complete support system.

Draw a mind map or make notes in your planner as to how you might enlist support from your fellow colleagues, parents/guardians, and some of your students.

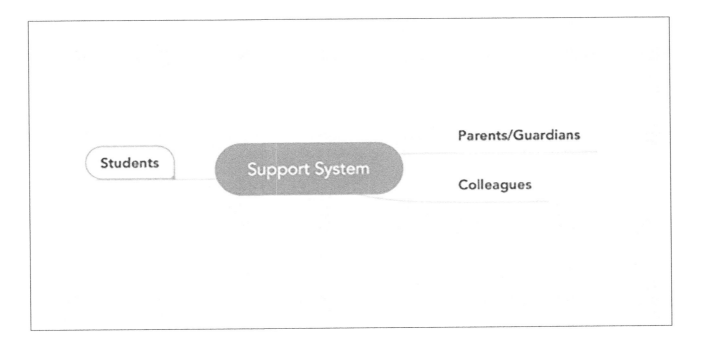

NOTES:

_____

_____

_____

_____

_____

_____

_____

_____

_____

_____

_____

_____

_____

_____

_____

_____

_____

_____

_____

_____

_____

_____

_____

_____

_____

2. ESTABLISHING ROUTINES

Resources

Take Control of the Noisy Class   Pages: 33–40

Additional resources

Needs Focused Classroom Management Video pack.   Videos 17–19: Routines
SAVE £150–Discounted access for workbook buyers.
Get the videos in digital form here for just £47 (normally £197):
https://needsfocusedteaching.com/video-packwbd

Key concepts

- Routines provide students with consistency and a clear route to behavioural success.

- They ensure students know what to do, when to do it, and how to do it.

- Most classroom problems can be prevented by having well-practised routines in place.

- Establishing routines will allow your classroom the opportunity to run smoothly and with less wasted time and energy.

- Routines enable students to take responsibility for their actions and their learning.

Focus Questions

1. What are the benefits of having routines in place? (p 33)

2. We (adults and children) regularly follow routines in everyday life. Give some examples of day-to-day routines and think how life would be different without them.

3. What are the 3 steps to setting up a new routine in the classroom and what should you be careful to avoid when creating a number of new routines? (pp 35-38)

4. How should the question "What should you be doing right now?" be used in conjunction with a well-rehearsed routine? (p 37)

5. What could you do to ensure all students follow a new routine? (pp 38-39)

6. How might you ensure a routine is maintained while also preparing for unstructured times and unplanned glitches during lessons? (pp 39-40)

7. Even though the focus of this chapter is not explicitly about learning, why are the ideas in this chapter essential for student learning?

8. Besides saving instructional time, what might be some other benefits of having a routine-based system in place for distributing materials at the start of a lesson?

9. What routines would you want students to adopt as a habit to carry through their school life?

10. How can you collaborate with other teachers to help reinforce a routine?

Activities

ACTIVITY 5 – The Need for Routines

Think of activities, transitions and times throughout a typical school day that involve a change to normal/current activities, that students take too long to accomplish, or that would benefit from having a system in place to help students know exactly what to do. These times and activities tend to lead to disruption, so we think of them as behaviour 'Hot Spots'. They are things like getting on the minibus, going on a trip, visiting the library, going to assembly, changing activity, watching a video, linking up for dinner/break, finishing work early, arriving to class late, group work, taking part in a discussion etc.

Write your classroom behaviour 'Hot Spots' here....

ACTIVITY 6 – Creating Routines

There are five key routines every teacher should have in place as a minimum on their journey to having an automated classroom:

Essential Routine #1: What students should do at the start of the lesson

Essential Routine #2: How students should appropriately seek help or support

Essential Routine #3: How materials and equipment are accessed

Essential Routine #4: How materials and equipment are put away

Essential Routine #5: What students should do at the end of the lesson

Use the information on pages 35-40 to create these routines, each having approximately 4-6 easy to follow steps. When writing your routines, be sure to phrase each step positively – the routine should explain what to do rather than what *not* to do.

Essential Routine #1: What students should do at the start of the lesson

_____

_____

_____

_____

_____

_____

Essential Routine #2: How students should appropriately seek help or support

_____

_____

_____

_____

_____

_____

Essential Routine #3: How materials and equipment are accessed

_____

_____

_____

_____

_____

_____

Essential Routine #4: How materials and equipment are put away

_____

_____

_____

_____

_____

_____

Essential Routine #5: What students should do at the end of the lesson

_____

_____

_____

_____

_____

_____

Share your ideas

Share your routines (and any others you create) in the **Classroom Management Success FB group** with a heading: **'Routine Ideas'**.

You can join the group here:
https://www.facebook.com/groups/Classroommanagementsuccess

ACTIVITY 7 – Implementing routines

Now it's time to start teaching and establishing routines in your classroom. Using the information on pages 36-40 to help you, fill out the following table for your first planned routine.

Remember: You should only teach one routine at a time to your students. Once this has become embedded as a habit, move on to the next routine.

When will I teach it?	
What steps will I use to teach it?	
How will I rehearse it with my students?	
How will I reinforce it?	
How will I monitor and assess its effectiveness?	

ACTIVITY 8 – Dealing with resistance

Resistance to a new routine is normal. Use the information on pages 38-39 to create a toolbox of methods and strategies you might use to increase cooperation.

Ways to ensure students buy in to classroom routines

NOTES:

_____

_____

_____

_____

_____

_____

_____

_____

_____

_____

_____

_____

_____

_____

_____

_____

_____

_____

_____

_____

_____

_____

_____

_____

_____

3. GIVING CLEAR INSTRUCTIONS

Resources

Take Control of the Noisy Class   Pages: 41-50

Additional Resources

Needs Focused Classroom Management Video pack.   Videos 5–7: Clear Communication
SAVE £150–Discounted access for workbook buyers.
Get the videos in digital form here for just £47 (normally £197):
https://needsfocusedteaching.com/video-packwbd

Key concepts

- In a learning-oriented environment, using clear communication helps students to understand what is expected and how to succeed.

- Effective communication does not just happen – it requires planning and effort to ensure complete understanding.

- Miscommunication creates confusion and misunderstanding, both of which are detrimental to a student's performance and self-esteem.

- A confused child will be more likely to misbehave and will be distracted from learning the material.

Additional Reading

Here is an example of how distorted communication can affect a young student.

Sarah, a young student, is excited about her first day of school. She can't wait to meet her teacher and find out what friends she will have in her class. Sarah is a bright, motivated and well-behaved little girl. She arrives on her first day and meets her teacher, Ms Smith, who is new, inexperienced and unsure of herself. While introducing herself to her new students, Ms Smith quickly skims over the classroom rules. One of the rules she has implemented is that if a student is late to class, they must first go to the office and sign in before coming to the classroom, and bring a note from the office signifying that they have signed in.

The rule is clumsily worded, and Sarah is confused. She is afraid to call attention to herself and does not ask for clarification regarding Ms Smith's classroom rules.

A few weeks pass and Sarah is enjoying being a student in Ms Smith's classroom. She feels a positive rapport with her teacher and is working extremely hard to learn all she can. One morning Sarah's mother is late dropping her off at school. Sarah feels anxious that she is late and runs straight to her classroom. Ms Smith, frustrated that Sarah comes in the classroom without a note from the office, frowns at Sarah when she arrives late and reprimands her for not following the classroom rule of signing in at the office first. Sarah becomes very embarrassed and confused since she was not aware of this classroom rule. She begins to cry and feels embarrassed that her teacher is yelling at her in front of the entire class.

The example of Sarah not understanding the class policy seems minor, but can have a ripple effect into her perception of her teacher and class as a whole.

If Sarah is confused regarding class policies, she will most likely become confused with future directions given by Ms Smith. The next time Sarah misunderstands directions the consequences could be more serious, further damaging her self-esteem and creating unnecessary conflict within the classroom.

Often children do not disobey class rules and regulations because they are 'naughty', although there are always those children who are, and deliberately disobey their teacher. It is common that children who do not fully understand class policy or instructions for certain classroom activities are unable to comply, since they are unaware of what they can and cannot do.

In the example of Sarah, a well-meaning student broke a class rule due to ineffective communication by the teacher. Sarah did not do anything 'wrong' since she was not aware of what she was supposed to do in the first place. Her shamed reaction to being scolded by her teacher is understandable. If she understood the classroom rules, she would most likely do everything possible to follow those rules to avoid confrontation and embarrassment. The misunderstanding caused by unclear communication created unnecessary drama and turmoil for both Sarah and her teacher that could have easily been avoided if clear communication had been implemented.

Focus Questions

1. Why do you think that 75% of communication is non-verbal? Provide some examples of non-verbal communication you use on a daily basis. (pp 41-43)

2. What are some ways that your messages are currently being misinterpreted by students or staff? (p 42)

3. Why is demonstrating a phrase or term, such as the appropriate volume for an indoor voice, beneficial and effective for students? (p 45)

4. How can asking questions, instead of giving clear directions, cause confusion for students? (p 49)

Activities

ACTIVITY 9 – Turning questions into directions

Simple and concise directions, delivered calmly and deliberately, are much more effective than questions if you want students to meet your expectations as explained on pages 49-50. Turn the following questions in directions or closed requests.

a. Can you please be quiet?

_____

b. Do you think you should be swinging on your chair like that?

_____

c. Will you please stop doing that? (to two students talking during independent work)

_____

d. Why do I need to keep asking you to turn around?

_____

e. Are you listening to me?

_____

f. Why are you doing that? (to a student scribbling on their work)

_____

g. Is anyone listening to me?

_____

h. Don't you think it would be a good idea to stop that? (to a student talking out of turn)

_____

i. What is wrong with you? (to a student continually avoiding work)

_____

ACTIVITY 10 – Giving instructions that students will follow

Use the information on pages 43-50 to rewrite instructions 1-5 below. Use at least two of the methods listed to make each instruction more effective.

- Confirmation of instructions

- Provide a reason

- Closed requests

- "When you do this... that happens" statements

1. "Complete tasks 1-5."

2. "Stop talking and get on with your work, please."

3. "There's too much noise. Quieten down!"

4. "Look at the mess you've made. Get it cleaned up."

5. "Stop it and get on with your work!"

Share your ideas

Share your reworded instructions in the **Classroom Management Success FB group** with a heading: **'Giving instructions that students will follow'**.

You can join the group here:
https://www.facebook.com/groups/Classroommanagementsuccess

NOTES:

_____

_____

_____

_____

_____

_____

_____

_____

_____

_____

_____

_____

_____

_____

_____

_____

_____

_____

_____

_____

_____

_____

_____

_____

_____

4. CONSEQUENCES

Resources

Take Control of the Noisy Class   Pages: 51-76

Additional resources

Needs Focused Teaching YouTube videos

Consequences (from the original *Take Control of the Noisy Class* web class):
https://youtu.be/zHbpxH4MAW0

How to use consequences to stop behaviour problems:
https://youtu.be/Jn9jcZilc7w

Videos 28 & 29 in the Needs Focused Classroom Management Video Pack
SAVE £150–Discounted access for workbook buyers.
Get the videos in digital form here for just £47 (normally £197):
https://needsfocusedteaching.com/video-packwbd

Key concepts

- Warnings and consequences should always be followed through.

- The right consequence, correctly applied, can help a teacher gain respect and build bonds with tough students.

- Correctly applied, consequences can bring a near-instant end to behaviour incidents by providing a clear, definite end-point the student understands.

- A hierarchy of stepped consequences enables a teacher to manage behaviour at class-room level.

Focus Questions

1. Why is it important to deliver consequences in stepped fashion? (p 53)

2. What does the term 'manage behaviour at classroom level' mean? Why is it important for a teacher to be able to do this?

3. Is it ever appropriate to "jump" steps when delivering consequences? If yes, provide an explanation.

4. What do you see as the benefits of The Two Minute Follow-Up as a general consequence and how might this contribute towards a long-term classroom management solution? (p 56)

5. Why is it important to take a student's personality, circumstances or history into consideration when delivering consequences, and how might this be done without flouting a teacher's need for consistency? (p 57)

6. What are some methods you can use to 'keep your cool' if you feel your emotions spiralling? (p 58)

7. How does offering a choice help students to think about their behaviour? (p 60)

8. What are some effective methods for stopping yourself from being pulled into secondary behaviours and backchat with a student when issuing consequences? (p 69-70)

Additional Reading

This explains how to devise suitable consequences.

In order to draw up a range of suitable consequences for use in the classroom it's important to first make the distinction between a consequence and a punishment. This important contrast will have an important bearing on our actions and the result of applying them.

The difference lies mainly with the intent. With a consequence the aim is to teach the student a lesson—in a fair and understanding manner. What we want is for our students to learn to make better decisions. A suitable consequence can be viewed as somewhat more considerate and perhaps even more lenient than a punishment; it's very much about being inconvenient rather than harmful. That said, inconvenient doesn't mean 'permissive'; we're still upholding and reinforcing boundaries, but we focus more on the certainty as opposed to the severity—the certainty that it will be followed through.

With a punishment the purpose is often to ridicule, embarrass, humiliate, or even cause harm—with little regard given to whether or not a better course of action has been discovered. Punishment doesn't promote or teach good behaviour; it merely says, 'don't do that!' and does nothing to clarify the how and why of appropriate action or what to do instead.

If we want behaviour to improve, we need to develop responsibility in our young. External control through punishment, rewards and bribes simply takes it away from them. Rewards (and bribes for that matter) simply take it away from them.As you'll see from the following examples, we can use consequences to teach responsibility and accountability. They help teach the behaviour we want to see—and without provoking retaliation from students (and their classmates in the audience) who view our treatment unfair or unjust.

So let's now look at some examples of appropriate consequences. As explained on page 58 of Take Control of the Noisy Class, the formula that I use to arrive at a suitable consequence is:

Suitable Consequence = Behaviour Problem + Restricted Access

In other words, a suitable consequence generally involves removal of, or limited access to, whatever was causing the problem.

Below are some examples of logical consequences devised using this formula.

EXAMPLE #1 Misuse of equipment: Restrict access for a short while.

"Stop swinging on your chair. If you do it again, I'll take your chair away and you can sit on the floor/stand for ten minutes."

"You know you're not supposed to wear a hat in school. Put it in your bag or it goes in my bag until the end of school."

"Put your headphones away or I will keep them in my locker until the end of the day."

EXAMPLE #2 Wasting time: *Take away some of their time.*

"Vicky, you are 3 minutes late for the lesson. You will be leaving 3 minutes after everyone else."

"Simon, you've wasted 5 minutes of lesson time. You will return at the start of break time to catch up work for 5 minutes."

EXAMPLE #3 Behaving inappropriately: *Have them spend their time practising appropriate behaviour.*

"Daniel, you were told not to run in the corridor. You can spend break time practising walking instead of running."

"All 5 of you have taken far too long to line up quietly. Come to my room at the start of break and we'll spend 10 minutes practising."

EXAMPLE #4 Messing around with other students: *Separate them from their peers.*

"You've shown me that you can't work sensibly as part of your group. You can sit next to me and work on your own for the next 10 minutes. When you've managed to do that, I'll let you return to the group. I'll set a timer."

Activities

ACTIVITY 11 – Logical consequences

Using the information above together with that on pages 51-76, complete the table below listing appropriate consequences for the stated behaviours.

Behaviour	Consequence or warning
Jonny is wasting time in your lesson despite having been given a warning.	
Jonny is 5 minutes late for the start of the lesson.	

Behaviour	Consequence or warning
Jonny continues to run in the corridor despite being warned about doing so.	
Jonny arrives at class wearing a hat.	
Jonny is swinging on his chair.	
Jonny has been disruptive during a group work session. He was warned that he would be separated from his group, but he continued to mess around. This is the initial warning Jonny was given: *"Jonny, when you mess about it makes it difficult for your group members to complete the task. If you can't remain in your seat and complete the task, you'll have to work on your own at the front."*	

ACTIVITY 12 – Creating a hierarchy of stepped consequences

Pages 53-57 and 61-66 of *Take Control of the Noisy Class* explain the benefits of stepped consequences and provide examples of their use in the classroom. In this activity you're going to get into the habit of structuring consequences in a stepped manner so that you can maintain control even when student misbehaviour escalates beyond the first warning. The secret is to start small so that you always have multiple options available to you.

Create a series of consequences, starting with a suitable warning and ending with a 'Top Tier Sanction' such as the Ten Minute Detention, or another of your choice, for the following behaviour problems. NB Leave the space marked 'Delivery Note' blank for now—you'll be adding to that later, in the next exercise.

Problem #1: Students talking inappropriately

Warning:

Delivery note _____

Consequence 1:

Delivery note _____

Consequence 2:

Delivery note _____

Top Tier Sanction:

Delivery note _____

Problem #2: Your choice – an issue you face regularly in class

Warning:

Delivery note _____

Consequence 1:

Delivery note _____

Consequence 2:

Delivery note _____

Top Tier Sanction:

Delivery note _____

Problem #3: Your choice – an issue you face regularly in class

Warning:

Delivery note _____

Consequence 1:

Delivery note _____

Consequence 2:

    Delivery note _____

Top Tier Sanction:

    Delivery note _____

ACTIVITY 13 – Delivering Consequences

Pages 57-60 and 66-73 explain how to deliver consequences effectively and without causing confrontation. Use this information to add notes about the delivery of your own consequences, as identified in Activity 12 above. Add these next to the 'delivery note' prompt.

ACTIVITY 14 – Secondary behaviours and backchat

It can be difficult to not get drawn into secondary behaviours—the mutterings, grumblings, insults and actions thrown out by frustrated students in their bid to have the last word and continue an argument. These are particularly prevalent during the issuing of consequences.

In this activity you're going to develop the habit of being able to rise above these behaviours with one, single, stock response that does not engage or provoke further reaction.

The main thrust of this response is this: 'Case Closed.' Whatever you say at this time should be concise and to the point, should be delivered in a matter-of-fact tone and should convey that you have finished dealing with this particular matter. Depending on the circumstances, an opportunity for the student to discuss things with you *later*—in their free time—can also be offered, if that seems fair and appropriate.

A useful response when students try to engage you in an argument by insulting you starts like this: *"That may be true, but…"*

For example:
Student: "Your lessons are crap. The work's boring."
Teacher: *"That may be true, but* right now you need to finish the task you've been given. You can come and see me to suggest some ways to make the lessons more appealing at break time if you like but for now, complete your work target."

Use this idea together with the suggestions on page 69 to help you write your own responses to the following comments:

That's not fair!	
Why are you always picking on me?	
This is stupid.	
She started it, not me. Punish her too.	
Prove that I did it.	
I want to talk to the principal.	
You didn't care when Steve did it.	
I hate you.	
Why are you making such a big deal out of this?	

Share your ideas

Share your ideas for dealing with backchat in the **Classroom Management Success FB group** with a heading: **'How to stop backchat'.**

You can join the group here:
https://www.facebook.com/groups/Classroommanagementsuccess

NOTES:

5. POSITIVE TEACHER-STUDENT RELATIONSHIPS: THE SECRET TO SUCCESSFUL CLASSROOM MANAGEMENT

Resources

Take Control of the Noisy Class   Pages: 77-104

Additional resources

Needs Focused Teaching YouTube videos:
https://www.youtube.com/watch?v=ZRzAopo3wAM
https://www.youtube.com/watch?v=r3RZ-s41Gxc

Needs Focused Classroom Management Video Pack
SAVE £150—Discounted access for workbook buyers.
Get the videos in digital form here for just £47 (normally £197):
https://needsfocusedteaching.com/video-packwbd

Key Concepts

- The key to effective classroom management is a positive teacher-student relationship.

- Taking the time and putting in the effort to cultivate and maintain positive relationships with students conveys the message, "I value you as a person".

- The expectations you have of your students will greatly influence their behaviour and achievement.

Focus Questions

1. What are the two essential factors suggested in *Take Control of the Noisy Class* for building positive relationships with students–fast? (p 81)

2. What is the main determining factor for frequent communication with your students and what are 3 ways you could facilitate this? (pp 81-87)

3. Why does asking students for advice help to create stronger relationships? (p 88)

4. What is 'The Franklin Effect' and how might you integrate it into your classroom practice to build positive connections with some of your students? (pp 89-90)

5. How does placing massive expectations of behaviour upon students help with effective classroom management? (p 93) How can you show a student that you are actively listening and engaged in the conversation? (p 99)

6. What is one new skill that you could share with your students to empower them and gain their trust? (p 101)

7. Think back to one of your favourite teachers. How might you emulate the actions and characteristics of this teacher with your own students?

8. Why do you think seemingly small gestures, such as saying "please" and "thank you" to your students, make such a big difference to your relationship with them?

9. What expectations do you have for your students? How do you convey those expectations to them?

Activities

ACTIVITY 15 – Initiating conversations – asking for advice:

Use the information on pages 87-98 of *Take Control of the Noisy Class* to help you prepare a quick list of topics on which you might ask a student for advice, as a means of breaking the ice with them.

1. _____

2. _____

3. _____

4. _____

5. _____

ACTIVITY 16 – Initiating conversations–asking a favour:

Use the information on pages 89-90 of *Take Control of the Noisy Class* to help you prepare a quick list of things you ask a student for help with.

1. _____

2. _____

3. _____

4. _____

5. _____

Share your ideas

Share your ideas for initiating conversations with students in the **Classroom Management Success FB group** with a heading: **'Initiating conversations with students'**.

You can join the group here:
https://www.facebook.com/groups/Classroommanagementsuccess

ACTIVITY 17 – Showing Students You Care:

Using pages 91-104 of *Take Control of the Noisy Class* as well as ideas of your own, list 10 ways you could show your students you care about them. You might find it helpful to think in terms of their welfare, their health, their happiness, their safety and their success.

1. _____

2. _____

3. _____

4. _____

5. _____

6. _____

7. _____

8. _____

9. _____

10. _____

Share your ideas

Share your ideas for showing students you care about them in the **Classroom Management Success FB group** with a heading: **'Showing students you care'**.

You can join the group here:
https://www.facebook.com/groups/Classroommanagementsuccess

ACTIVITY 18 – Finding students' interests and passions

Pages 83-87 of *Take Control of the Noisy Class* outline the importance of getting to know your students better and finding out their interests and passions. This is an extremely important part of the relationship-building process.

What other 'under the radar' ways can you think of, other than The Record Card Questionnaire and the Suggestion Box, to discover your students' interests?

Method #1: _____

Method #2: _____

Method #3: _____

ACTIVITY 19 – The Record Card Questionnaire

Print out a copy of the Record Card Questionnaire from your resource area:
www.noisyclass.com/bookresources

Edit the questionnaire to suit the age group and needs of your students and put it in to operation as soon as possible.

ACTIVITY 20 – Communicating frequently

Besides having face-to-face conversations with students, how else might you communicate with your students so as to convey the fact you care about them? Try to think of at least five different methods.

1. _____
2. _____
3. _____
4. _____
5. _____

Share your ideas

Share these ideas in the **Classroom Management Success FB group** with a heading: 'Frequent communication with students'

You can join the group here:
https://www.facebook.com/groups/Classroommanagementsuccess

NOTES:

_____
_____
_____
_____
_____
_____
_____
_____
_____
_____
_____
_____
_____
_____
_____
_____
_____
_____
_____
_____
_____
_____
_____
_____
_____
_____
_____

6. POSITIVE REINFORCEMENT

Resources

Take Control of the Noisy Class   Pages: 105-130

Additional resources

Needs Focused teaching YouTube video: Praise:
https://www.youtube.com/watch?v=N1FToUWFquY

Needs Focused Classroom Management Video Pack
SAVE £150–Discounted access for workbook buyers.
Get the videos in digital form here for just £47 (normally £197):
https://needsfocusedteaching.com/video-packwbd

Key concepts

- Looking for, focusing on, and acknowledging *good* behaviour, rather than being on the lookout for inappropriate behaviour, is a fast and powerful way to create positive changes in the classroom.

- Positive reinforcement creates a ripple effect of positive feelings which in turn lead to positive choices being made by students.

Focus Questions

1. Why might it be helpful to use praise to encourage effort instead of waiting until the completion of a task? (p 112)

2. What are some ways that you can ensure that your praise is sincere and not a generic statement? (pp 112-113).

3. What is one simple change you can make in your delivery of praise to make it more effective in your classroom? (p 113)

4. "What two factors explained on pages 110-111 will make praise more effective by conveying to a student that you fully recognise their efforts? How might we guide students to reflect on their efforts to encourage them further? (p 113) What is one form of non-verbal reinforcement that you would like to trial in your own classroom? (pp 119-121)

5. What are some of the biggest challenges around offering material rewards to students on a long term basis? (p 122)

6. What are some effective ways you can offer rewards to students so that they still hold meaning? (p 123)

7. Which of the classroom privileges, found on pages 125-128, would blend well into your current classroom?

Activities

ACTIVITY 21 – Create a Praise Wall

It can be difficult, when juggling the responsibilities of a full-time teacher, to remember to praise students, despite all the benefits of doing so. One method to help recognise a student's good behaviour or accomplishments is something known as a Praise Wall. You can call it whatever you want—in my room it was known as 'The Wall of Fame'—but essentially this is simply a place to acknowledge your students' efforts publicly. Keep in mind that some students may not want public praise—at least not at first. Give them the option of having their work or effort displayed anonymously on the board and acknowledge them in private. In time they may well want to have their accomplishments properly acknowledged with a label bearing their name.

To make the board you just need a space on a wall in your classroom; you can ask some of your students to decorate it with a border and a fancy title. Next, you share with students that when you notice them doing something nice, helping out or just being deserving of praise, you will write this down and place it, with their name, on the board.

The Praise Wall can be changed as often as you want and has the added benefit of giving the students a place to recognise their fellow students' efforts, too. Continually adding to the board like this can quickly help create a very supportive, caring classroom community.

Share your ideas

Share your pictures in the **Classroom Management Success FB group** with a heading: 'My Praise Wall'

You can join the group here:
https://www.facebook.com/groups/Classroommanagementsuccess

ACTIVITY 22 – The Right Rewards

On pages 125-130 of *Take Control of the Noisy Class* you'll find suggestions for different types of rewards. After reading these, consult pages 122-125 about the correct way to use rewards, and fill in the table below with some reward suggestions of your own; these should be suited to your particular students and educational setting.

Classroom privileges	Special awards and trophies	Work-related awards	Trips and excursions

Classroom privileges	Special awards and trophies	Work-related awards	Trips and excursions

Share your ideas

Share your ideas in the **Classroom Management Success FB group** with a heading: 'Classroom Reward Ideas'

You can join the group here:
https://www.facebook.com/groups/Classroommanagementsuccess

ACTIVITY 23 – Effective praise

Using the information on pages 109-122 in *Take Control of the Noisy Class*, read through the following scenarios and provide a suitably effective praise statement or method.

Scenario	Effective Praise
Tammy and Amy have been working together all morning. Tammy has been helping Amy by sharing some examples of her work and helping her with the more complex questions. This is the best Amy has done all year on an assignment.	
Rhonda has a habit of acting up and causing disruptions in class. You decide to assign a task to Rhonda to hand out and collect papers as each section of the lesson is completed. You are surprised that Rhonda has been behaving positively the entire lesson.	
Danny, who can be a troublemaker, has been helping another boy in the classroom. You noticed that the other boy has been picked on by other kids and that Danny appears to have made a connection with him.	
Sarah has been having outbursts in class, which seems to be out of character for her. As the day continues, you notice that Sarah has finally quietened down after you speak with her about her behaviour and some issues she has had at home.	
Upon entering the classroom, you see that one of your students, Tom, has cleaned up his messy area from the day before without being asked.	

NOTES:

7. TAKING CONTROL AT THE DOOR

Resources

Take Control of the Noisy Class   Pages: 133-138

Additional resources

Needs Focused Teaching YouTube videos:
https://www.youtube.com/watch?v=u086rr7SRso&t=392s

Needs Focused Classroom Management Video Pack
SAVE £150–Discounted access for workbook buyers.
Get the videos in digital form here for just £47 (normally £197):
https://needsfocusedteaching.com/video-packwbd

Key concepts

- Classroom management starts outside the classroom.

- Difficult groups need to be settled gradually.

Focus Questions

1. What are the advantages of spending time with your students at the door? (pp 134-136)

2. What are some things you might want to look for in students that may create problems in your lesson? (pg. 136)

3. How long should you spend on the process of calming students down at the door? (p 138)

Activities

ACTIVITY 24 – Non-confrontational statements

Pages 134-135 of *Take Control of the Noisy Class* introduce the idea of making non-confrontational statements to students about the behaviour you expect from them. This process is also explained in the YouTube video tutorial mentioned above in the additional resources.

It's a good idea to plan in advance the behaviours you want and expect your students to display at the door, and to consider the statements you will make to reinforce and encourage these behaviours. In the box below write down at least 5 non-confrontational statements you might use with your students:

ACTIVITY 25 – Informal Chit-chat

Pages 135-138 of *Take Control of the Noisy Class* explain the importance of chatting informally with your students prior to letting them into the classroom. This is also explained in the YouTube video tutorial mentioned above in the additional resources. What type of questions will you ask and what things will you chat about with your students at the door? Write them in the box below.

ACTIVITY 26 – Kid Culture

Effective teaching hinges upon communication, and you can't communicate without entering into the world of those you wish to reach. Being up-to-date with pop culture makes it much easier to connect with young people. This activity is about becoming more familiar with the kind of topics your students are likely to be interested in, and devising ways you can integrate these topics into your teaching. Complete the table below with specific examples of pop culture your students are known to engage with.

NB You will find this exercise a LOT easier if you first complete the exercises in section 5 above.

Topics for you to explore	How you might involve these in teaching

Topics for you to explore	How you might involve these in teaching

NOTES:

8. SEATING PLANS

Resources

Take Control of the Noisy Class   Pages: 139-144

Additional resources

Needs Focused Classroom Management Video Pack
SAVE £150–Discounted access for workbook buyers.
Get the videos in digital form here for just £47 (normally £197):
https://needsfocusedteaching.com/video-packwbd

Key Concepts

* A seating plan is an essential tool for reducing behaviour problems and improving student engagement.One of the best ways to reduce behaviour problems and improve participation during lessons is to seat students in table groups.

Focus Questions

1. Describe the specific grouping associated with cooperative learning teams. (pp 141-142)

2. How might you deal with complaints from students about a particular seating plan? (p 141)

3. What are the four main benefits to grouping your students in cooperative learning teams (p 142)

Activities

ACTIVITY 27 – A 4-step Seating Plan

Write a simplified 4-step plan for grouping your students into cooperative learning teams using the information on pages 143-144 of *Take Control of the Noisy Class* to help you.

Step #1: _____

_____

_____

_____

_____

Step #2: _____

_____

_____

_____

_____

Step #3: _____

_____

_____

_____

_____

Step #4: _____

_____

_____

_____

_____

NOTES:

9. GETTING THEM INTO THE ROOM – THE FILTER METHOD

Resources

Take Control of the Noisy Class   Pages: 145-152

Additional resources

Needs Focused Teaching YouTube videos:
https://www.youtube.com/watch?v=u086rr7SRso&t=392s

Needs Focused Classroom Management Video Pack
SAVE £150–Discounted access for workbook buyers.
Get the videos in digital form here for just £47 (normally £197):
https://needsfocusedteaching.com/video-packwbd

Key Concepts

- The filter method enables you to minimise classroom behaviour problems before the lesson starts by establishing a positive tone, getting the bulk of your (responsive) students into your classroom in an orderly fashion, and by identifying and addressing students who need more attention to help them settle.

Focus Questions

1. What are some key words and phrases that you can use to move students from 'play-time' to 'work-time'? (p 145)

2. Why is it important to separate the students who listen from the non-listeners? (p 147) What are some starter activities that you can use for the students who are listening to keep them engaged? (p 149)

3. What are some considerations you need to make when leaving one student in a corridor alone? (p 152)

Activities

ACTIVITY 28 – YOUR Filter Method

Write down the 6 steps of the filter method briefly, in your own words, so that you are completely familiar with the process.

Step #1: _____

_____

_____

_____

_____

Step #2: _____

_____

_____

_____

_____

Step #3: _____

_____

_____

_____

_____

Step #4: _____

_____

_____

_____

_____

Step #5: _____

_____

_____

_____

_____

Step #6: _____

_____

_____

_____

_____

NOTES:

10. GETTING THE LESSON STARTED

Resources

Take Control of the Noisy Class   Pages: 153-166

Additional resources

Needs Focused Classroom Management Video Pack
SAVE £150–Discounted access for workbook buyers.
Get the videos in digital form here for just £47 (normally £197):
https://needsfocusedteaching.com/video-packwbd

The Fun Teacher's Tool kit: Hundreds of Ways to Create a Positive Classroom Environment & Make Learning FUN (Needs Focused Teaching Resource Book 4). Available on Amazon.

Attention-Grabbing Starters & Plenaries for Teachers: 99 Outrageously Engaging Activities to Increase Student Participation and Make Learning Fun (Needs Focused Teaching Resource Book 2). Available on Amazon.

Key Concepts

The first five minutes will dictate how the lesson will continue and conclude, so it is important to get your lesson started in the right manner.

- There are four main ways to start a lesson, and the method you use should reflect the types of students in your classroom (as well as your own personality).

Focus Questions

1. Why is the start of a lesson an important time to set the tone? (p 153)

2. What are the main features of each of the four lesson starts?

3. Which of the four starting methods do you find the most appealing, and why?

4. What are some possible disadvantages to the 'fun start' approach, and how can you work to ensure that they don't become a problem? (p 161)

5. How can you ensure that your questions are engaging for students? (p 165)

6. How might you transition from a formal start to a more engaging start?

7. Write down the main features of each of the four lesson starts.

Formal Start	Settled Start	Fun Start	Engaging Question Start

Activities

ACTIVITY 29 – Create a 'Settled Start' schedule.

In this activity you'll plan the first 5-15 minutes of a lesson in the form of a generic 'settled start' so that you can adapt it to specific subjects or topics as needed. Use the following questions to help you.

Q. What activity/activities will you provide the students to keep them focused during this period?

Q. Will you provide a choice of activity?

Q. How do you plan to explain the activity? On the board; verbally; or with handouts?

Q. Do you plan to provide the students with feedback or assessment on the activity? How?

Q. What time limit or completion target will you set?

Q. How do you plan to reinforce the learning that is taking place?

Q. What routines, in terms of acceptable behaviour, do you hope to establish and reinforce during this period? (For example: seating, accessing resources, noise levels etc.) See pages 33-40 for more information on routines.

Q. How do you plan to transition into your main teaching activity?

Settled Start Plan

```
Settled Start Plan




















```

ACTIVITY 30 – Create a 'Fun Start' schedule

In this activity you'll plan the first 5-15 minutes of a lesson in the form of a generic 'fun start' so that you can adapt it to specific subjects or topics as needed. Use the following questions to help you.

Q. What activity or activities will you provide the students to keep them focused during this period?

Q.   Will you provide a choice of activity?

Q. How do you plan to explain the activity? On the board; verbally; or with handouts?

Q. Do you plan to provide the students with feedback or assessment on the activity? How?

Q. What time limit or completion target will you set?

Q. How do you plan to reinforce the learning that is taking place?

Q. What routines, in terms of acceptable behaviour, do you hope to establish and reinforce during this period? (For example: seating, accessing resources, noise levels etc.) See pages 33-40 for more information on routines.

Q. How do you plan to transition into your main teaching activity?

Fun Start Plan

NOTES:

_____

_____

_____

_____

_____

_____

_____

_____

_____

_____

_____

_____

_____

_____

_____

_____

_____

_____

_____

_____

_____

_____

_____

_____

_____

11. MAINTAINING A POSITIVE LEARNING ENVIRONMENT

Resources

Take Control of the Noisy Class   Pages: 167-191

Additional resources

Needs Focused Classroom Management Video Pack
SAVE £150–Discounted access for workbook buyers.
Get the videos in digital form here for just £47 (normally £197):
https://needsfocusedteaching.com/video-packwbd

The Fun Teacher's Tool kit: Hundreds of Ways to Create a Positive Classroom Environment & Make Learning FUN (Needs Focused Teaching Resource Book 4). Available on Amazon.

Attention-Grabbing Starters & Plenaries for Teachers: 99 Outrageously Engaging Activities to Increase Student Participation and Make Learning Fun (Needs Focused Teaching Resource Book 2). Available on Amazon.

Key Concepts

- Providing engaging and interactive lesson activities is one of the simplest ways to reduce behaviour problems in the classroom. It's easy to make a lesson more engaging–by ensuring some or all of the features in this section are implemented.

Focus Questions

1. Why is it important to ensure work is both achievable and appropriate to a student's ability? How might you do this in your lessons? (pp 172-174)

2. What are some methods you can use to reignite curiosity with students who may have become disengaged from the lesson or topic? (p 170)

3. In what ways might you use props to extend or expand learning in your subject? (pp 178-179)

4. How can providing students with choices enhance their learning and behaviour? (p 181)

5. Do you feel that the material that you are currently delivering is relevant to the students? If not, how could you modify it to make it relevant? (pp 181-183)

6. In what ways might it be beneficial to provide students with opportunities to teach each other? (p 191)

Activities

ACTIVITY 31 – Appealing Lessons

Read through the ideas from pages 171-191 and complete the table below for a future lesson.

	Appealing Lesson Checklist	
Genuine Praise	What opportunities will there be to praise students? What can you do to ensure your students' efforts are acknowledged?	

	Appealing Lesson Checklist	
Achievable & Appropriate Tasks	How will you make sure you pitch tasks at appropriate ability levels so as not to overwhelm your students while still giving them an acceptable level of challenge?	
Music & Sound Effects	Will you play music to mark transitions, settle the class or as a classroom management tool?	
Props	What props will you use to illustrate teaching points or make the lesson more fun?	

	Appealing Lesson Checklist	
Variety of activities	What sort of activities will you provide? Will you include pair work/ group work?	
Choice	Will you give your students an element of choice? How?	
Relevance	How will you make the work relevant to your students?	

	Appealing Lesson Checklist	
Teach Backs & Reviews	What consolidation activities will you put in place?	

NOTES:

12. MAINTAINING LESSON FLOW

Resources

Take Control of the Noisy Class   Pages: 193-215

Additional resources

Needs Focused Classroom Management Video Pack
SAVE £150–Discounted access for workbook buyers.
Get the videos in digital form here for just £47 (normally £197):
https://needsfocusedteaching.com/video-packwbd

The Fun Teacher's Tool kit: Hundreds of Ways to Create a Positive Classroom Environment & Make Learning FUN (Needs-Focused Teaching Resource Book 4). Available on Amazon.

Attention-Grabbing Starters & Plenaries for Teachers: 99 Outrageously Engaging Activities to Increase Student Participation and Make Learning Fun (Needs Focused Teaching Resource Book 2). Available on Amazon.

Key Concepts

- Momentum helps to reduce behaviour problems.

- Breaks are a useful way to refocus student attention and regain momentum.

Focus Questions

1. What are some ways to create structured breaks that don't require a lot of time to get students back on track? (p 194)

2. How can you chunk lessons to allow students a more digestible curriculum? (p 199)

3. In what ways does creating timelines or measurable outcomes help to create a clear learning path for students? (p 200)

4. What are some methods for producing the instructions at the beginning of the lesson so that you don't have to continuously interrupt the students? (p 201)

5. How can using the question, "How can you feel supported right now?" change the atmosphere of the classroom? (p 201)

Activities

ACTIVITY 32 – Create your emergency activity stockpile

As explained on page 194 of *Take Control of the Noisy Class*, having a collection of 'emergency' activities on hand can be especially useful to occupy bored, tired or frustrated students. Spend a few hours putting together a pack of differentiated task sheets with which to engage your students next time a planned activity or task doesn't work out. You may find the two books mentioned above in the additional resources helpful.

ACTIVITY 33 – Work Targets and Support

As explained on pages 199-200 of *Take Control of the Noisy Class*, work targets are incredibly effective for keeping students engaged in independent work and/or refocusing them when they start to engage in off-task behaviours.

Take a look at a piece of work you have set for a mixed ability class and make quick notes of the work targets you could issue to various students. Take special note of the 'Hot Tip' box on page 200.

ACTIVITY 34 – Gaining Student Attention

Page 205 of *Take Control of the Noisy Class* provides 23 suggestions to get a class's attention. In this activity you will choose three activities to try with your classroom. It is important to keep in mind that you don't want to make too many changes at once for the students—changes need to be made gradually and over an extended period of time. This means that when you choose three activities, you may only want to start with one and trial it for a week or two to see how the students react. Use the following observation chart:

Chosen Activity	Summary after first introduction to the class	Observations after seven days of using the activity

NOTES:

13. DEALING WITH PROBLEMS

Resources

Take Control of the Noisy Class   Pages: 217-249

Additional Resources

The Classroom Management Tool Kit: Behaviour Solutions for Today's Tough Classrooms (Needs Focused Teaching Resource Book 6) Available on Amazon.

Classroom Management Success in 7 Days or Less: The Ultra-Effective Classroom Management System for Teachers (Needs Focused Teaching Resource, Book 1) Available on Amazon or get a FREE copy by attending the web class below.

Free Online Classroom Management Web Tutorial with Rob Plevin:
https://needsfocusedteaching.lpages.co/cm-webinar-generic/

If the link above isn't working, go here:
www.needsfocusedteaching.com/web-session

Focus Questions

1. What are some common distractions or interruptions that your students are experiencing most often? How can you plan to change activities without causing a lot of extra planning on your part? (p 220)

2. What is the difference between a limited choice and a confrontational command? (p 221)

3. How can you create clear boundaries and expectations for students when it comes to inappropriate behaviour? (p 224)

4. Why is it important to develop clear consequences early on, rather than trying to implement them later? (p 227)

5. How can you include peers and parents in the planning process for homework to ensure that students are more motivated to complete it? (p 232-234)

6. How do you currently deal with students who are coming late to class? How can you use the methods suggested on pages 240-242 to help with this issue?

Activities

ACTIVITY 35 – Responding to problems

In this activity you will create a set of responses you'll be able to use for the most problematic and frequently-occurring behaviour problems in your classroom.

Start by making a list of the behaviour issues you are most likely to face with your teaching groups. Write them in the table below in the column labelled 'Behaviour problem'.

Based on everything you've learned in *Take Control of the Noisy Class* and the associated resources, choose responses you feel would be most suitable for each problem. Add them to your table in the 'Solutions' column. Chapter 13 of *Take Control of the Noisy Class* includes a number of responses to most common classroom behaviour problems—use this section to help you.

Behaviour problem	Solutions

Behaviour problem	Solutions

ACTIVITY 36 – The Clean Slate

In this activity, you're going to plan out how you could approach 'starting over' with an extremely difficult class. Using any of the information and resources you have learned over the course of *Take Control of the Noisy Class*, especially the information on pages 245-249, put together a stepped plan to get this group back on side.

Step #1 – Break their routine

How might you get the attention of this group and get them to listen to you?

How will you arrange the classroom?

What could you put in place to break their usual negative state and make them more attentive?

Step #2 – Group discussion

What questions do you plan to raise?

How will you record the students' views?

What rules will you have for this discussion?

What consequences will you have in place for those who break the rules and how will you enforce them?

Step #3–Follow-up

How will you distribute the conclusions from the discussion? How will you ensure the points raised are acted upon?

ACTIVITY 37 – Reflection

Q. What are the three biggest key takeaways from the book for you–that you would share immediately with other teachers?

Q. How has your perspective of classroom management changed over the course of this workbook?

Q. How has your classroom tone changed as you implemented changes?

Q. What was one activity that you were surprised worked with your students?

Q. How could you take some of the activities to the next level with your students?

Post-course Activity

Complete this table to compare your starting point and assess your progress now that you have completed the workbook.

REVIEW ASSESSMENT:

My progress as a Needs Focused teacher

Rank each statement by circling a number between 1 (low) and 10 (high).

I have a positive attitude towards my students and my teaching	1 2 3 4 5 6 7 8 9 10
I have routines in place to automate my classroom and make transitions run smoothly	1 2 3 4 5 6 7 8 9 10
I make a priority of building positive relationships with my students and making each of them feel valued	1 2 3 4 5 6 7 8 9 10
I focus on positive classroom management by acknowledging and praising appropriate behaviour	1 2 3 4 5 6 7 8 9 10
I have high expectations for all my students	1 2 3 4 5 6 7 8 9 10
My students are calm and settled at the start of my lessons	1 2 3 4 5 6 7 8 9 10
I make sure to give clear instructions, in a calm manner, phrased so that my students will understand them	1 2 3 4 5 6 7 8 9 10
I know how to establish and maintain a positive learning environment	1 2 3 4 5 6 7 8 9 10
I know how to maintain lesson flow in order to minimise disruption and misbehaviour	1 2 3 4 5 6 7 8 9 10
I know how to deliver consequences without causing animosity	1 2 3 4 5 6 7 8 9 10
I have a range of specific responses for the most common classroom behaviour problems	1 2 3 4 5 6 7 8 9 10
I know how to start over with a very difficult class.	1 2 3 4 5 6 7 8 9 10

APPENDIX

Suggested Study Group Activities

Group Activity #1: The Hot Seat

The Hot Seat is a wonderful resource for a teacher looking for help with a specific behaviour or teaching problem.

The natural tendency of most professionals when attempting to help a colleague is to give advice. And no matter how well-meaning this advice may be, it can unfortunately make the recipient feel incapable.

The Hot Seat is designed to make problem solving more productive so that group members can seek help without feeling their skills are in question.

The Hot Seat Process

The Study Group Leader (SGL) will follow the process described in the following sections to help the Study Group utilise the expertise of the group members *as well as* the teacher in the Hot Seat (hereby known as 'The Hot Seater'). After all, this teacher knows the student and the problem better than anyone else in the group and is therefore the real expert in the group—they just need help to draw out that knowledge and expertise.

i) *Identify the problem*

The Hot Seater describes the problem to study group members in sufficient detail to enable group members to gain a good understanding of the problem and difficulties being faced.

ii) *Describe attempts to solve the problem*

Following clarification of the problem, the SGL will ask the Hot Seater to explain the ways they've attempted to solve the problem to date, making special note of any strategies that have led to improvements.

iii)   Group brainstorming

The SGL will now call on the group members to suggest possible solutions to the problem by asking them to describe attempts to solve similar problems in the past using a prompt such as:

"Has anybody in the group ever faced a student/group/situation like this? If so, what things did you try, even if they were only partially successful?" Once all suggestions arising from direct experience have been offered, a second round of ideas is generated by asking group members for other possible solutions that do not come directly from classroom experience.

"Does anybody have any other ideas for solving this problem that perhaps don't come from experiences that you have had in the classroom?"

The SGL may also contribute but they must wait until last.

iv)   Planning

In the planning phase the Hot Seater gets to decide on their ideal intervention plans and processes for implementation in the coming days or weeks. The SGL might prompt this by asking: *"On the basis of all that's been offered, what seems most helpful to you, and how do you plan to implement it?"* The plan should be described in full detail at this time, when the specifics of the situation are clear to everyone.

v)   Follow-up

The final stage is to follow up with Hot Seater with regard to progress, and for the group to help with any difficulties that have cropped up during implementation.

Group Activity #2: Peer Observation

One of the greatest barriers to professional development in teaching is the fact that most teachers operate in a 'feedback vacuum' with few opportunities available to watch and learn directly from others, or to gain feedback on one's own practice. Peer observation is a powerful and effective tool for the enhancement of teaching skills (provided it forms part of a collaborative, supportive process) by enabling teachers to learn from each other's practice.

The following guidelines will help ensure peer observation is supportive, comfortable and productive.

1) Team with a colleague whom you like, trust and respect.

2) Decide who will play the part of teacher, and who will be the observer.

3) Plan the lesson together and decide on a focus for the observation.

4) The observer makes detailed notes on a minute-by-minute basis, with feedback being non-judgmental and non-evaluative.

5) During post-lesson feedback the observer starts by telling the teacher what they liked about the lesson, and asks them about the lesson in terms of: their ideas for development; anything they would have done differently; and where the lesson would sit in a whole scheme of work. This is done *before* the observer gives their feedback and supportive suggestions for improvement.

Group Activity #3: Role Play

Study group members will volunteer to play the roles of:

1) one or more disruptive students and

2) the teacher. Additional roles might include support assistants and other non-teaching staff members, depending on the scenario for the role play. Scenarios are decided by the study group members depending on school or department-specific needs. The *coach* will describe the upcoming scene so that colleagues playing the role of students will know exactly how to behave in character.

Tip: Have an agreed signal to indicate when everyone is to be 'in character' and 'out of character' so that feedback and discussion can take place in a sensible, professional manner. The role play can thus be safely halted at any time.

Coaching

There are two main choices for coaching within the framework of the role play. In the first, the coach will model for the teacher exactly what to do as they walk everyone through the scene. Thus the modelling provides a dry run for the teacher so that the routine will have been rehearsed immediately prior to the role play. In the second, the entire study group (including role play participants) discusses the problems associated with the scenario. Together they then agree on a planned intervention for the teacher to implement during the role play.

Playing out the scene

During the role play of the scene, as the teacher deals with the students' misbehaviour, the coach and group members watch closely.

The scene can be replayed several times, using prompts and suggestions from the group as a whole, until everyone is satisfied that the intervention is as good as it can be.

Feedback

The first stage of the feedback phase is for the coach to describe the strengths of the teacher's performance. Opportunity is then given to the teacher to give their opinion on their own performance. If the teacher is aware of some deficit in performance, it is better that he or she describe it to the group than *vice versa*. Usually the teacher will also describe what they plan to do differently the next time, due to insight they gained from the role playing.

Feedback from other participants—the disruptive students in particular—is vital throughout this process.; it can often give insight as to how relevant parties might be feeling during intervention.

Made in the USA
Las Vegas, NV
27 March 2024

87848412R00052